May your hot flashes be more like
tropical vacations
and less like hellish infernos

Menopause Made Me do it, or Forget To Do it!
Funny Notebook and Daily Planner for Menopausal Women
Published by: Hot Mama Material
original pub. date 8/31/2021 revised/updated 10/10/2021
Printed by Amazon
Made in the USA
ISBN-13#979-8468118641

GET THINGS DONE!

TOP PRIORITIES FOR THE DAY	CHORES	WATER

- cleaning up
- make the bed
- laundry
- wash the dishes
- feed the pets

1X250ML

TO-DO	THINGS TO DO TOMORROW	FOOD

BREAKFAST | LUNCH | DINNER

APPOINTMENTS

PHONE /EMAIL

FITNESS

NOTES

MOOD SKETCH

GET THINGS DONE!

TOP PRIORITIES FOR THE DAY	CHORES	WATER
	cleaning up wash the dishes make the bed feed the pets laundry	1X250ML

TO-DO | THINGS TO DO TOMORROW | FOOD

| | | BREAKFAST | LUNCH | DINNER |

APPOINTMENTS | PHONE / EMAIL

FITNESS | NOTES

MOOD SKETCH

GET THINGS DONE!

TOP PRIORITIES FOR THE DAY	CHORES	WATER
	cleaning up wash the dishes make the bed feed the pets laundry	1x250ML

TO-DO	THINGS TO DO TOMORROW	FOOD
		BREAKFAST | LUNCH | DINNER
	APPOINTMENTS	PHONE /EMAIL
FITNESS	NOTES	
		MOOD SKETCH

GET THINGS DONE!

TOP PRIORITIES FOR THE DAY	CHORES	WATER
	cleaning up wash the dishes make the bed feed the pets laundry	1x250ML

TO-DO | THINGS TO DO TOMORROW | FOOD

| BREAKFAST | LUNCH | DINNER |

APPOINTMENTS | PHONE /EMAIL

FITNESS | NOTES

MOOD SKETCH

GET THINGS DONE!

TOP PRIORITIES FOR THE DAY	CHORES	WATER
	cleaning up wash the dishes make the bed feed the pets laundry	1X250ML

TO-DO | THINGS TO DO TOMORROW | FOOD

BREAKFAST | LUNCH | DINNER

APPOINTMENTS | PHONE /EMAIL

FITNESS | NOTES

MOOD SKETCH

GET THINGS DONE!

TOP PRIORITIES FOR THE DAY	CHORES	WATER

- cleaning up
- wash the dishes
- make the bed
- feed the pets
- laundry

7X250ML

TO-DO	THINGS TO DO TOMORROW	FOOD

BREAKFAST | LUNCH | DINNER

APPOINTMENTS

PHONE /EMAIL

FITNESS

NOTES

MOOD SKETCH

GET THINGS DONE!

TOP PRIORITIES FOR THE DAY	CHORES	WATER
	cleaning up wash the dishes make the bed feed the pets laundry	10x250ML

TO-DO	THINGS TO DO TOMORROW	FOOD
		BREAKFAST LUNCH DINNER

	APPOINTMENTS	PHONE /EMAIL

FITNESS	NOTES	
		MOOD SKETCH

GET THINGS DONE!

TOP PRIORITIES FOR THE DAY

CHORES

- cleaning up
- wash the dishes
- make the bed
- feed the pets
- laundry

WATER

1x250ML

TO-DO

THINGS TO DO TOMORROW

FOOD

BREAKFAST | LUNCH | DINNER

APPOINTMENTS

PHONE /EMAIL

FITNESS

NOTES

MOOD SKETCH

GET THINGS DONE!

TOP PRIORITIES FOR THE DAY	CHORES	WATER
	cleaning up wash the dishes make the bed feed the pets laundry	1X250ML

TO-DO	THINGS TO DO TOMORROW	FOOD
		BREAKFAST / LUNCH / DINNER
	APPOINTMENTS	PHONE / EMAIL
FITNESS	NOTES	
		MOOD SKETCH

GET THINGS DONE!

TOP PRIORITIES FOR THE DAY	CHORES	WATER

CHORES:
- cleaning up
- wash the dishes
- make the bed
- feed the pets
- laundry

1X250ML

TO-DO	THINGS TO DO TOMORROW	FOOD

BREAKFAST | LUNCH | DINNER

APPOINTMENTS

PHONE / EMAIL

FITNESS

NOTES

MOOD SKETCH

GET THINGS DONE!

TOP PRIORITIES FOR THE DAY	CHORES	WATER
	cleaning up / wash the dishes / make the bed / feed the pets / laundry	1X250ML

TO-DO	THINGS TO DO TOMORROW	FOOD
		BREAKFAST / LUNCH / DINNER

	APPOINTMENTS	PHONE / EMAIL

FITNESS	NOTES	
		MOOD SKETCH

GET THINGS DONE!

TOP PRIORITIES FOR THE DAY

CHORES
- cleaning up
- wash the dishes
- make the bed
- feed the pets
- laundry

WATER

1X250ML

TO-DO

THINGS TO DO TOMORROW

FOOD
| BREAKFAST | LUNCH | DINNER |

APPOINTMENTS

PHONE /EMAIL

FITNESS

NOTES

MOOD SKETCH

GET THINGS DONE!

TOP PRIORITIES FOR THE DAY	CHORES	WATER

CHORES:
- cleaning up
- wash the dishes
- make the bed
- feed the pets
- laundry

1X250ML

TO-DO | THINGS TO DO TOMORROW | FOOD

BREAKFAST | LUNCH | DINNER

APPOINTMENTS | PHONE /EMAIL

FITNESS | NOTES

MOOD SKETCH

GET THINGS DONE!

TOP PRIORITIES FOR THE DAY	CHORES	WATER

- cleaning up
- make the bed
- laundry
- wash the dishes
- feed the pets

1X250ML

TO-DO | THINGS TO DO TOMORROW | FOOD

BREAKFAST | LUNCH | DINNER

APPOINTMENTS | PHONE /EMAIL

FITNESS | NOTES

MOOD SKETCH

GET THINGS DONE!

TOP PRIORITIES FOR THE DAY

CHORES

- cleaning up
- wash the dishes
- make the bed
- feed the pets
- laundry

WATER

1X250ML

TO-DO

THINGS TO DO TOMORROW

FOOD

BREAKFAST	LUNCH	DINNER

APPOINTMENTS

PHONE / EMAIL

FITNESS

NOTES

MOOD SKETCH

GET THINGS DONE!

TOP PRIORITIES FOR THE DAY	CHORES	WATER

CHORES:
- cleaning up
- make the bed
- laundry
- wash the dishes
- feed the pets

1X250ML

TO-DO	THINGS TO DO TOMORROW	FOOD

BREAKFAST | LUNCH | DINNER

APPOINTMENTS | PHONE /EMAIL

FITNESS | NOTES

MOOD SKETCH

GET THINGS DONE!

TOP PRIORITIES FOR THE DAY	CHORES	WATER

CHORES
- cleaning up
- wash the dishes
- make the bed
- feed the pets
- laundry

WATER: 1X250ML

TO-DO	THINGS TO DO TOMORROW	FOOD

FOOD: BREAKFAST | LUNCH | DINNER

APPOINTMENTS

PHONE /EMAIL

FITNESS

NOTES

MOOD SKETCH

GET THINGS DONE!

TOP PRIORITIES FOR THE DAY	CHORES	WATER

CHORES
- cleaning up
- make the bed
- laundry
- wash the dishes
- feed the pets

1X250ML

TO-DO	THINGS TO DO TOMORROW	FOOD

BREAKFAST | LUNCH | DINNER

APPOINTMENTS

PHONE / EMAIL

FITNESS

NOTES

MOOD SKETCH

GET THINGS DONE!

TOP PRIORITIES FOR THE DAY	CHORES	WATER
	cleaning up wash the dishes make the bed feed the pets laundry	1X250ML

TO-DO | THINGS TO DO TOMORROW | FOOD

BREAKFAST   LUNCH   DINNER

APPOINTMENTS | PHONE /EMAIL

FITNESS | NOTES

MOOD SKETCH

GET THINGS DONE!

TOP PRIORITIES FOR THE DAY	CHORES	WATER

CHORES:
- cleaning up
- wash the dishes
- make the bed
- feed the pets
- laundry

1X250ML

TO-DO	THINGS TO DO TOMORROW	FOOD

BREAKFAST | LUNCH | DINNER

APPOINTMENTS

PHONE /EMAIL

FITNESS

NOTES

MOOD SKETCH

GET THINGS DONE!

TOP PRIORITIES FOR THE DAY	CHORES	WATER
	cleaning up wash the dishes make the bed feed the pets laundry	1X250ML

TO-DO

THINGS TO DO TOMORROW

FOOD

BREAKFAST	LUNCH	DINNER

APPOINTMENTS

PHONE /EMAIL

FITNESS

NOTES

MOOD SKETCH

GET THINGS DONE!

TOP PRIORITIES FOR THE DAY	CHORES	WATER

cleaning up — wash the dishes
make the bed — feed the pets
laundry

1X250ML

TO-DO	THINGS TO DO TOMORROW	FOOD

BREAKFAST | LUNCH | DINNER

APPOINTMENTS — PHONE /EMAIL

FITNESS — NOTES

MOOD SKETCH

GET THINGS DONE!

TOP PRIORITIES FOR THE DAY	CHORES	WATER
	cleaning up wash the dishes make the bed feed the pets laundry	1X250ML

TO-DO | THINGS TO DO TOMORROW | FOOD

BREAKFAST | LUNCH | DINNER

APPOINTMENTS | PHONE /EMAIL

FITNESS | NOTES

MOOD SKETCH

GET THINGS DONE!

TOP PRIORITIES FOR THE DAY	CHORES	WATER

CHORES:
- cleaning up
- make the bed
- laundry
- wash the dishes
- feed the pets

1X250ML

TO-DO	THINGS TO DO TOMORROW	FOOD

BREAKFAST | LUNCH | DINNER

APPOINTMENTS | PHONE / EMAIL

FITNESS | NOTES

MOOD SKETCH

ET THINGS DONE!

TOP PRIORITIES FOR THE DAY	CHORES	WATER
	cleaning up wash the dishes make the bed feed the pets laundry	1X250ML

TO-DO	THINGS TO DO TOMORROW	FOOD
		BREAKFAST LUNCH DINNER

	APPOINTMENTS	PHONE / EMAIL

FITNESS	NOTES	
		MOOD SKETCH

GET THINGS DONE!

TOP PRIORITIES FOR THE DAY	CHORES	WATER

CHORES:
- cleaning up
- wash the dishes
- make the bed
- feed the pets
- laundry

1X250ML

TO-DO	THINGS TO DO TOMORROW	FOOD

BREAKFAST | LUNCH | DINNER

APPOINTMENTS

PHONE / EMAIL

FITNESS

NOTES

MOOD SKETCH

GET THINGS DONE!

TOP PRIORITIES FOR THE DAY	CHORES	WATER
	cleaning up — wash the dishes make the bed — feed the pets laundry — ___ — ___	(10 glasses) 1X250ML

TO-DO

THINGS TO DO TOMORROW

FOOD
BREAKFAST	LUNCH	DINNER

APPOINTMENTS

PHONE /EMAIL

FITNESS

NOTES

MOOD SKETCH

GET THINGS DONE!

TOP PRIORITIES FOR THE DAY	CHORES	WATER
	cleaning up wash the dishes make the bed feed the pets laundry	1X250ML

TO-DO	THINGS TO DO TOMORROW	FOOD
		BREAKFAST LUNCH DINNER

	APPOINTMENTS	PHONE / EMAIL

FITNESS	NOTES	
		MOOD SKETCH

GET THINGS DONE!

TOP PRIORITIES FOR THE DAY	CHORES	WATER
	cleaning up wash the dishes make the bed feed the pets laundry	1X250ML

TO-DO	THINGS TO DO TOMORROW	FOOD
		BREAKFAST LUNCH DINNER

	APPOINTMENTS	PHONE / EMAIL

FITNESS	NOTES	
		MOOD SKETCH

GET THINGS DONE!

TOP PRIORITIES FOR THE DAY	CHORES	WATER
	cleaning up wash the dishes make the bed feed the pets laundry	1X250ML

TO-DO	THINGS TO DO TOMORROW	FOOD
		BREAKFAST LUNCH DINNER

	APPOINTMENTS	PHONE /EMAIL

FITNESS	NOTES	
		MOOD SKETCH

GET THINGS DONE!

TOP PRIORITIES FOR THE DAY	CHORES	WATER
	cleaning up wash the dishes make the bed feed the pets laundry	1X250ML

TO-DO	THINGS TO DO TOMORROW	FOOD
		BREAKFAST LUNCH DINNER

	APPOINTMENTS	PHONE / EMAIL

FITNESS	NOTES	

		MOOD SKETCH

GET THINGS DONE!

TOP PRIORITIES FOR THE DAY	CHORES	WATER

CHORES:
- cleaning up
- make the bed
- laundry
- wash the dishes
- feed the pets

1X250ML

TO-DO	THINGS TO DO TOMORROW	FOOD

BREAKFAST | LUNCH | DINNER

APPOINTMENTS | PHONE /EMAIL

FITNESS | NOTES

MOOD SKETCH

GET THINGS DONE!

TOP PRIORITIES FOR THE DAY	CHORES	WATER
	cleaning up wash the dishes make the bed feed the pets laundry	1X250ML

TO-DO

THINGS TO DO TOMORROW

FOOD

BREAKFAST	LUNCH	DINNER

APPOINTMENTS

PHONE / EMAIL

FITNESS

NOTES

MOOD SKETCH

GET THINGS DONE!

TOP PRIORITIES FOR THE DAY	CHORES	WATER
	cleaning up wash the dishes make the bed feed the pets laundry	1X250ML

TO-DO

THINGS TO DO TOMORROW

FOOD

BREAKFAST	LUNCH	DINNER

APPOINTMENTS

PHONE /EMAIL

FITNESS

NOTES

MOOD SKETCH

GET THINGS DONE!

TOP PRIORITIES FOR THE DAY	CHORES	WATER
	cleaning up wash the dishes make the bed feed the pets laundry	1X250ML

TO-DO	THINGS TO DO TOMORROW	FOOD
		BREAKFAST LUNCH DINNER

	APPOINTMENTS	PHONE / EMAIL

FITNESS	NOTES	
		MOOD SKETCH

GET THINGS DONE!

TOP PRIORITIES FOR THE DAY	CHORES	WATER
	cleaning up — wash the dishes make the bed — feed the pets laundry —	(10 glasses) 1X250ML

TO-DO | THINGS TO DO TOMORROW | FOOD

| BREAKFAST | LUNCH | DINNER |

APPOINTMENTS | PHONE / EMAIL

FITNESS | NOTES

MOOD SKETCH

GET THINGS DONE!

TOP PRIORITIES FOR THE DAY	CHORES	WATER
	cleaning up wash the dishes make the bed feed the pets laundry	1X250ML

TO-DO	THINGS TO DO TOMORROW	FOOD
		BREAKFAST LUNCH DINNER

	APPOINTMENTS	PHONE / EMAIL

FITNESS	NOTES	

MOOD SKETCH

GET THINGS DONE!

TOP PRIORITIES FOR THE DAY	CHORES	WATER
	○ cleaning up ○ wash the dishes ○ make the bed ○ feed the pets ○ laundry ○ _____ ○ _____ ○ _____	1x250ML

TO-DO	THINGS TO DO TOMORROW	FOOD
		BREAKFAST | LUNCH | DINNER
	APPOINTMENTS	PHONE /EMAIL
FITNESS	NOTES	
		MOOD SKETCH

GET THINGS DONE!

TOP PRIORITIES FOR THE DAY	CHORES	WATER
	cleaning up · wash the dishes make the bed · feed the pets laundry ·	1X250ML

TO-DO	THINGS TO DO TOMORROW	FOOD
		BREAKFAST · LUNCH · DINNER

	APPOINTMENTS	PHONE / EMAIL

FITNESS	NOTES	
		MOOD SKETCH

GET THINGS DONE!

TOP PRIORITIES FOR THE DAY	CHORES	WATER
	cleaning up — wash the dishes make the bed — feed the pets laundry — ___	1X250ML

TO-DO	THINGS TO DO TOMORROW	FOOD
		BREAKFAST | LUNCH | DINNER
	APPOINTMENTS	PHONE /EMAIL
FITNESS	NOTES	
		MOOD SKETCH

GET THINGS DONE!

TOP PRIORITIES FOR THE DAY	CHORES	WATER
	cleaning up wash the dishes make the bed feed the pets laundry	1X250ML

TO-DO | THINGS TO DO TOMORROW | FOOD

| | | BREAKFAST | LUNCH | DINNER |

APPOINTMENTS | PHONE / EMAIL

FITNESS | NOTES

MOOD SKETCH

GET THINGS DONE!

TOP PRIORITIES FOR THE DAY	CHORES	WATER

CHORES:
- cleaning up
- wash the dishes
- make the bed
- feed the pets
- laundry

1X250ML

TO-DO	THINGS TO DO TOMORROW	FOOD

BREAKFAST | LUNCH | DINNER

APPOINTMENTS

PHONE / EMAIL

FITNESS

NOTES

MOOD SKETCH

GET THINGS DONE!

TOP PRIORITIES FOR THE DAY	CHORES	WATER
	cleaning up wash the dishes make the bed feed the pets laundry	1X250ML

TO-DO

THINGS TO DO TOMORROW

FOOD

BREAKFAST	LUNCH	DINNER

APPOINTMENTS

PHONE / EMAIL

FITNESS

NOTES

MOOD SKETCH

GET THINGS DONE!

TOP PRIORITIES FOR THE DAY	CHORES	WATER
	cleaning up · wash the dishes make the bed · feed the pets laundry · _____	1X250ML

TO-DO	THINGS TO DO TOMORROW	FOOD
		BREAKFAST · LUNCH · DINNER

	APPOINTMENTS	PHONE /EMAIL

FITNESS	NOTES	
		MOOD SKETCH

GET THINGS DONE!

TOP PRIORITIES FOR THE DAY	CHORES	WATER
	cleaning up wash the dishes make the bed feed the pets laundry	1X250ML

TO-DO

THINGS TO DO TOMORROW

FOOD

BREAKFAST	LUNCH	DINNER

APPOINTMENTS

PHONE / EMAIL

FITNESS

NOTES

MOOD SKETCH

GET THINGS DONE!

TOP PRIORITIES FOR THE DAY	CHORES	WATER
	cleaning up wash the dishes make the bed feed the pets laundry	1X250ML

TO-DO	THINGS TO DO TOMORROW	FOOD
		BREAKFAST LUNCH DINNER

	APPOINTMENTS	PHONE /EMAIL

FITNESS	NOTES	

MOOD SKETCH

GET THINGS DONE!

TOP PRIORITIES FOR THE DAY	CHORES	WATER
	cleaning up wash the dishes make the bed feed the pets laundry	1X250ML

TO-DO | THINGS TO DO TOMORROW | FOOD

| | | BREAKFAST | LUNCH | DINNER |

APPOINTMENTS | PHONE / EMAIL

FITNESS | NOTES

MOOD SKETCH

GET THINGS DONE!

TOP PRIORITIES FOR THE DAY	CHORES	WATER

- cleaning up
- wash the dishes
- make the bed
- feed the pets
- laundry

1X250ML

TO-DO	THINGS TO DO TOMORROW	FOOD

BREAKFAST | LUNCH | DINNER

APPOINTMENTS | PHONE /EMAIL

FITNESS | NOTES

MOOD SKETCH

GET THINGS DONE!

TOP PRIORITIES FOR THE DAY	CHORES	WATER
	cleaning up wash the dishes make the bed feed the pets laundry	1X250ML

TO-DO	THINGS TO DO TOMORROW	FOOD
		BREAKFAST | LUNCH | DINNER

	APPOINTMENTS	PHONE / EMAIL

FITNESS	NOTES	
		MOOD SKETCH

GET THINGS DONE!

TOP PRIORITIES FOR THE DAY	CHORES	WATER
	cleaning up wash the dishes make the bed feed the pets laundry	1X250ML

TO-DO	THINGS TO DO TOMORROW	FOOD
		BREAKFAST / LUNCH / DINNER

	APPOINTMENTS	PHONE / EMAIL

FITNESS	NOTES	
		MOOD SKETCH

GET THINGS DONE!

TOP PRIORITIES FOR THE DAY	CHORES	WATER

- cleaning up
- make the bed
- laundry
- wash the dishes
- feed the pets

1X250ML

TO-DO	THINGS TO DO TOMORROW	FOOD

BREAKFAST	LUNCH	DINNER

APPOINTMENTS

PHONE /EMAIL

FITNESS

NOTES

MOOD SKETCH

GET THINGS DONE!

TOP PRIORITIES FOR THE DAY	CHORES	WATER

- cleaning up
- make the bed
- laundry
- wash the dishes
- feed the pets

1X250ML

TO-DO	THINGS TO DO TOMORROW	FOOD

| | | BREAKFAST | LUNCH | DINNER |

APPOINTMENTS

PHONE / EMAIL

FITNESS

NOTES

MOOD SKETCH

GET THINGS DONE!

TOP PRIORITIES FOR THE DAY	CHORES	WATER
	cleaning up wash the dishes make the bed feed the pets laundry	1X250ML

TO-DO | THINGS TO DO TOMORROW | FOOD

BREAKFAST	LUNCH	DINNER

APPOINTMENTS | PHONE /EMAIL

FITNESS | NOTES

MOOD SKETCH

GET THINGS DONE!

TOP PRIORITIES FOR THE DAY	CHORES	WATER
	cleaning up — wash the dishes make the bed — feed the pets laundry	1X250ML

TO-DO | THINGS TO DO TOMORROW | FOOD

BREAKFAST | LUNCH | DINNER

APPOINTMENTS | PHONE / EMAIL

FITNESS | NOTES

MOOD SKETCH

GET THINGS DONE!

TOP PRIORITIES FOR THE DAY	CHORES	WATER
	cleaning up wash the dishes make the bed feed the pets laundry	1X250ML

TO-DO

THINGS TO DO TOMORROW

FOOD

BREAKFAST	LUNCH	DINNER

APPOINTMENTS

PHONE /EMAIL

FITNESS

NOTES

MOOD SKETCH

GET THINGS DONE!

TOP PRIORITIES FOR THE DAY	CHORES	WATER

Chores:
- cleaning up
- wash the dishes
- make the bed
- feed the pets
- laundry

1X250ML

TO-DO	THINGS TO DO TOMORROW	FOOD

BREAKFAST | LUNCH | DINNER

APPOINTMENTS

PHONE / EMAIL

FITNESS

NOTES

MOOD SKETCH

GET THINGS DONE!

TOP PRIORITIES FOR THE DAY	CHORES	WATER

CHORES:
- cleaning up
- wash the dishes
- make the bed
- feed the pets
- laundry

1X250ML

TO-DO	THINGS TO DO TOMORROW	FOOD

BREAKFAST | LUNCH | DINNER

APPOINTMENTS

PHONE /EMAIL

FITNESS

NOTES

MOOD SKETCH

GET THINGS DONE!

TOP PRIORITIES FOR THE DAY	CHORES	WATER

CHORES:
- cleaning up
- make the bed
- laundry
- wash the dishes
- feed the pets

1X250ML

TO-DO	THINGS TO DO TOMORROW	FOOD

FOOD: BREAKFAST | LUNCH | DINNER

APPOINTMENTS

PHONE /EMAIL

FITNESS

NOTES

MOOD SKETCH

GET THINGS DONE!

TOP PRIORITIES FOR THE DAY	CHORES	WATER
	cleaning up wash the dishes make the bed feed the pets laundry	1X250ML

TO-DO | THINGS TO DO TOMORROW | FOOD

BREAKFAST   LUNCH   DINNER

APPOINTMENTS | PHONE /EMAIL

FITNESS | NOTES

MOOD SKETCH

GET THINGS DONE!

TOP PRIORITIES FOR THE DAY	CHORES	WATER

CHORES:
- cleaning up
- wash the dishes
- make the bed
- feed the pets
- laundry

1X250ML

TO-DO	THINGS TO DO TOMORROW	FOOD

BREAKFAST | LUNCH | DINNER

APPOINTMENTS

PHONE /EMAIL

FITNESS

NOTES

MOOD SKETCH

GET THINGS DONE!

TOP PRIORITIES FOR THE DAY	CHORES	WATER
	cleaning up / wash the dishes / make the bed / feed the pets / laundry	1X250ML

TO-DO | THINGS TO DO TOMORROW | FOOD

| | | BREAKFAST | LUNCH | DINNER |

APPOINTMENTS | PHONE / EMAIL

FITNESS | NOTES

MOOD SKETCH

GET THINGS DONE!

TOP PRIORITIES FOR THE DAY	CHORES	WATER

CHORES:
- cleaning up
- make the bed
- laundry
- wash the dishes
- feed the pets

1X250ML

TO-DO	THINGS TO DO TOMORROW	FOOD

BREAKFAST | LUNCH | DINNER

	APPOINTMENTS	PHONE / EMAIL

FITNESS	NOTES	

MOOD SKETCH

GET THINGS DONE!

TOP PRIORITIES FOR THE DAY	CHORES	WATER
	cleaning up wash the dishes make the bed feed the pets laundry	1X250ML

TO-DO | THINGS TO DO TOMORROW | FOOD

| BREAKFAST | LUNCH | DINNER |

APPOINTMENTS | PHONE /EMAIL

FITNESS | NOTES

MOOD SKETCH

Printed by Amazon Italia Logistica S.r.l.
Torrazza Piemonte (TO), Italy